The Gools

Jean Ure

Illustrated by David Pattison

Chapter 1

This is a story about a family of Gools, who all lived together in a nest, in a churchyard, underneath a yew tree.

There was Granny Gool, and Grandpa Gool. There was Great Aunt Gertie Gool. There was Mummy Gool and Daddy Gool. There was Glenn Gool. There was Griselda Gool. And last of all there was Baby Gool.

If ever you walked in the churchyard in the daytime you would never guess that there were Gools about. In the daytime, Gools stay in their nests and sleep. It is at night-time that the fun begins!

As soon as the moon is in the sky, Gools rise from their beds and start gooling and ghosting. If you walk in the churchyard at night-time, you will see them for sure.

Before we go on, I must let you into a secret. Gools are harmless! They never hurt anyone. Not many people know this. Even grown-ups turn white as sheets and start running away when they see a Gool.

Gools think this is very funny.

"Heee haaa hoooo!" hoot the Gools, whenever they see someone running. Gools enjoy a good hoot.

"Hooo haaa heee!" goes Great Aunt Gertie Gool.

"Haaa hooo haaa!" goes Granny.

"Heeee hooo haaa!" wheezes Grandpa.

There is nothing Gools like better than to see someone running away. It is their idea of fun. To sca-a-a-are people RIGID ...

The only Gool that nobody ever ran away from was Baby Gool. Poor Baby Gool! He tried his very best. He hooted and he honked, he waggled his fingers and he crossed his eyes, but all people ever did was laugh.

He pulled a big, bad, ugly face at the vicar, and the vicar just smiled at him.

He jumped out of a tree and shouted "Boo!" at a cat, and the cat just yawned and went back to sleep.

Glenn and Griselda jeered.

Granny and Grandpa sighed.

Mummy and Daddy shook their heads.

Great Aunt Gertie went, "Tut tut!"

Nobody was frightened of him. He would never make a proper Gool!

Chapter 2

One winter's night when the moon was full, Mummy Gool said, "We are going to go out gooling. Baby had better stay at home."

Baby begged and pleaded to go with them, but nobody wanted him.

"I'm not going gooling with him!" said Griselda.

"He's too little," said Glenn. "People would laugh."

"Yes," said Griselda, "and that would spoil everything."

"Maybe when you're bigger you will be able to come," said Great Aunt Gertie, kindly.

"When he's learnt how to frighten people," said Griselda.

"I was frightening people when I was far younger than he is," boasted Glenn.

"So was I," said Griselda.

A tear went plopping down
Baby's cheek. Granny and Grandpa
saw it and felt sorry for him.

"Perhaps I will stay and keep him
company," said Grandpa. "I'm really
getting a bit old for all this gooling."

Granny reached into her store cupboard, beneath one of the roots of the yew tree. This was where she kept all her goodies.

"Here is a nice bag of bones," said Granny. "You play with those. We'll be back soon."

"Bye-bye! Be a good Gool," said Daddy.

Mummy kissed him and Great Aunt Gertie patted his cheek. Then off they all went, leaving Baby Gool with Grandpa.

"Heee hooo haaaa!" wheezed Grandpa. "This will be a good night for gooling!"

Baby Gool did wish that he could go with them! But he was too little. People would laugh.

Very soon the churchyard was full of strange noises.

"Hooo haaa hoo!" hooted Granny, flapping up and down.

"Oh ooh ah!" moaned Great Aunt Gertie.

Mummy and Daddy perched side by side on the gatepost. They were having a sing-song.

"Waaa ee ooh!" they sang. Mummy sang sharp and Daddy sang flat. It sounded more frightening that way.

Glenn was floating in mid-air, waiting to scare members of the choir.

Griselda was hiding behind a gravestone, pulling faces. In a moment she was going to jump out and shout "Wheeeeee!" at a boy and girl who were sitting on a seat.

Baby Gool felt so sad as he played with his bones.

"I wish I was a proper grown-up Gool that could scare people," he said.

"Zzzzzzz," said Grandpa, in reply. Grandpa Gool had gone to sleep! How could he sleep when so much fun was going on?

"Teee heee heee!" went Glenn, chasing choir boys down the path.

"Help! Help!" cried the boy and girl who were sitting on the seat.

Griselda popped up between them and shouted, "Wheeeee!" She had also pulled a truly horrible face. Now they were running away just as fast as they could.

"Gools!" they cried. "Help!"
"Help!" they cried. "Gools!"
"Zzzzzz," went Grandpa.

Baby pushed his bones away from him. He had made up his mind: he was too old to play with bones! He was going to go and be a real big grown-up Gool and scare somebody ...

Chapter 3

Holding his breath, Baby Gool shimmered past Grandpa and floated out into the churchyard.

An old lady was coming up the path with a small black-and-white dog. They were out for their evening stroll in the moonlight.

Baby Gool giggled to himself. Tee hee! Old ladies were easy to scare. He would scare the old lady!

Baby tucked himself away behind a bush and waited.

"Boo!" screamed Baby, chasing after them.

"What a lovely night," said the old lady to the dog. "How peaceful it is!"

"Boo!" screeched Baby, right into the old lady's ear. "Boo!" he bellowed. "Boo-OO-OOO!"

"Did I hear something?" wondered the old lady.

"Ugh! Boo! Boils and goo!" yelled Baby, bouncing up and down. The old lady looked round.

"Who is using naughty words?" she said.

"Me!" shouted Baby. "Me, me, me!"

The old lady shook her head and peered through her glasses. The dog didn't need glasses. He could see perfectly well without them. What he could see was a small fat Gool, jumping up and down.

"Haaa-ruff!" barked the dog.

Chapter 4

"Help!" squealed Baby Gool. Baby Gool turned and ran. The dog ran after him. Baby Gool sprang in terror up a tree. The dog barked excitedly. He had scared away a Gool!

Baby Gool sat on a branch and began to cry.

"Jumbo!" The old lady was coming back down the path, calling to her dog. "Where are you, you bad boy?"

The old lady stopped and peered up into the tree.

"Why, it's a little Gool!" she said. "Why are you weeping, little Gool?"

"Because I can't scare anybody!" blubbed Baby Gool.

"Because you can't scare anybody? But why ever would you want to?" asked the old lady, taking out her hanky and mopping at Baby Gool's eyes.

From all over the churchyard, heads were popping up. First Mummy Gool's, then Daddy Gool's, then Granny's, then Great Aunt Gertie's,

then Glenn's, then Griselda's. Even
Grandpa woke from his sleep. Their
eyes grew as round as dustbin lids.
Baby was talking to a human!

"Now, tell me," said the old lady. "Why do you want to scare people?"

Baby Gool put a thumb in his mouth.

"Don't know," he said. He had never stopped to think about it. Scaring people was what Gools did.

"Don't you think it would be far nicer," said the old lady, "if you made friends with them?"

Friends???

All over the churchyard, the Gools scratched their heads and stared.

Friends?

37

"Well," said Granny, "I suppose we could always *try* it."

"We could always *try* it," agreed Grandpa and Great Aunt Gertie.

"Yes!" cried Glenn and Griselda. "We can always *try* it!"

"All right," said Mummy and Daddy. "Let's try it! After all, it would be something new!"

Chapter 5

And so they tried it. And now, if you go into the churchyard at night-time, you will see all these jolly Gools, bobbing and beaming and being just as friendly as can be.

They have quite given up frightening people. Every now and again Granny might do a little moaning and wailing or Great Aunt Gertie might have a bit of a hoot, because Granny and Great Aunt Gertie are old and it is not easy for them to change their ways. But

Grandpa has retired and is taking things easy, and Mummy and Daddy are quite happy to sit on the gatepost in the evening and nod and smile at the passers-by.

Glenn and Griselda have taken up bell-ringing. This means that sometimes the bells start to ring when the vicar isn't expecting it, but he doesn't seem to mind. He laughs and tells people, "I have Gools in my belfry!"

As for Baby, he has become great pals with the old lady and her dog. He always joins them for their evening stroll and floats about the churchyard with them.

Last month was Baby's birthday and he had a birthday party to which everyone was invited. There was Granny Gool and Grandpa Gool, and Mummy Gool and Daddy Gool, and Great Aunt Gertie Gool, and Glenn Gool and Griselda Gool,

and the members of the choir, and
the old lady and the small dog, and
the Vicar, and the boy and the girl
who had sat on the seat, and the cat
that Baby had jumped out and said
"Boo" at.

They had a wonderful time! They played all sorts of party games such as hide-and-seek, and now-you-see-me-now-you-don't, and here-we-come-gathering-toadstools, and

clammy-hands-all-in-a-ring, and
eerie-feary-footsteps, and goose
bumps (which was won by the vicar).

It was the very best birthday party that Baby had ever had.
Making friends was *fun*!